Luke 17:3-4 (AMP) - Pay attention and always be on your guard [looking out for one another]. If your brother sins (misses the mark), solemnly tell him so and reprove him, and if he repents (feels sorry for having sinned), forgive him. And even if he sins against you seven times in a day, and turns to you seven times and says, I repent [I am sorry], you must forgive him (give up resentment and consider the offense as recalled and annulled).

Forgiveness is not optional or situational; it is mandatory.

-

Lorenzo T. Brown

Keon
Tannehill

MOVING BEYOND THE OFFENSE

LIVING WITHOUT ANIMOSITY

Lorenzo T. Brown

Is-Able *M*inistries
PMB 325
1919 Oxmoor Road
Birmingham, AL 35209

MOVING
BEYOND
THE
OFFENSE

LIVING WITHOUT ANIMOSITY

All scripture is from the New King James Version and Amplified Bible unless otherwise noted.

ISBN paperback 978-1-937908-41-6

ISBN electronic 978-1-937908-43-0

I would like to dedicate this book to my niece, Alicia; who was killed at 11-months-old. Losing you brought us all great pain. Our ability to forgive was truly tested when we had to face those who were responsible for taking your life. I know that you are resting in peace and smiling down from Heaven because we forgave those who took your life.

 LORENZO T. BROWN is the Founder of Is-Able Ministries, located in Birmingham, Alabama. He is a devoted husband and loving father. Lorenzo is a sought after inspirational speaker. His purpose is to inspire and encourage others to reach their full potential despite their circumstances. At the age of 17, he was shot. The bullet went in through the front of his neck, lodged inside his spinal cord and instantly paralyzed him from his chest down to his feet. In this book he shares his amazing journey of forgiveness, in hopes that all that are living in the bondage of unforgiveness will be set free.

www.isableministries.org

ALSO BY LORENZO T. BROWN

Vol. 1 Thirty-One Principles for Daily Living
(31-Day Devotional & Journal)

Vol. 1 Moments of Inspiration
(52-Week Devotional & Journal)

Contents

....

Preface   1

....

Introduction   3
We Can Only Move as Far as the Offense Will Allow Us

....

1. The Night My Life Changed   7

....

2. Going to the Nursing Home   23

....

3. Forgiving the Men Who Left Me Paralyzed   39

....

4. Forgiving My Parents   57

....

5. Forgiving My Family and Friends   71

....

6. Forgiving God   79

....

Closing Words   89

....

Acknowledgements   91

....

Questions and Topics for Discussion   93

MOVING BEYOND THE OFFENSE

Preface

....

Forgiveness has set me free to live. - Lorenzo T. Brown

Although I have changed the names to protect the privacy of some of the individuals in this book; everything you read is true. Forgiving someone who has offended you is a very difficult thing to do, but I have discovered that it is one of the most liberating and fulfilling deeds in the world.

Becoming paralyzed at the age of 17 was a difficult thing for me to accept and live with. It was even more difficult to forgive the men who were responsible for this and very difficult to forgive my family and friends for not being there when I needed them the most.

My hope and prayer is that every reader who has been offended by someone in any way will be able to learn from my journey, be empowered to move beyond the offense and live without animosity.

*This is my recollection of events. I am relating them to the best of my knowledge.

Introduction

We Can Only Move as Far as the Offense Will Allow Us.

....

Forgiveness does not mean that you are going to forget the act; forgiveness causes you to forget the effect of the act. - Lorenzo T. Brown

If you are human, you have more than likely been offended by someone at some point in your life. That person's wrong actions toward you caused you a lot of hurt and pain. It left you damaged and you probably struggled to get beyond the offense.

If someone did something wrong to you on January 30, 1980 or April 23, 1993, (whatever the date may be) and every time you talk or think about what happened to you on that date you begin to relive the pain, anger rises inside of you and a desire for revenge enters your heart; you are stuck at that date. We can only move as far as the offense will allow us.

Luke 17:3-5 (AMP) - "Pay attention and always be on your guard [looking out for one another]. If your brother sins (misses the mark), solemnly tell him so and reprove him, and if he repents (feels sorry for having sinned), forgive him. And even if he sins against you seven times in a day, and turns to you seven times and says, I repent [I am sorry], you must forgive him (give up resentment and consider the offense as recalled and annulled). The apostles said to the Lord, Increase our faith (that trust and confidence that spring from our belief in God)."

Notice the emphasis that Christ stresses here. He says, "You must forgive him." He did not say you only had to forgive if the offense was only minor. It does not matter if the offense was major or minor, forgiveness is not optional. We must forgive.

In verse 5, the apostles replied and said, "Lord, increase our faith." The apostles had been given power to cast out demons, speak with new tongues, take up serpents, drink deadly substances without harm and lay hands on the sick (Mark 16:17-18).Yet, when it came to forgiveness they asked the Lord to increase their faith. I have spoken with various pastors and I have researched Biblically-related books and websites and found that this is the only time the disciples requested an increase in faith. The disciples felt they needed an increase in faith in order to continually forgive.

Many of us probably feel the same way the disciples felt when it comes to forgiveness. One of the reasons why it is so difficult for us to forgive is because we think if we forgive the person who offended us, we are doing them a favor but forgiveness is not for the other person, forgiveness is for us; it sets us free.

A question that I am asked a lot is "Do you have to forget in order to forgive?" The answer is no. I was shot on June 26, 1994, and I can tell you every detail about what happened that night and I am never going to forget it. However, before I fully forgave, whenever I would talk or think about what happened on that date, I would relive the pain. Anger would rise inside of me and a desire for revenge would enter my heart; I was stuck at that date. Once I fully forgave, I was able to talk and think about that date without reliving the pain, without having anger rise inside of me or without having a desire for revenge to enter my heart; I was able to move beyond the offense.

Forgiveness does not mean that you are going to forget the act; forgiveness causes you to forget the effect of the act. You will no longer have to live captive to the other person's wrong actions toward you. You will not have to be resentful, bitter, live with unforgiveness or have a desire for revenge inside of your heart. You will no longer have to relive the pain. You can live free of animosity.

How do you recover from the damage and move beyond the offense? That is what I would like to teach you.

Chapter 1

The Night my Life Changed

....

Ephesians 4:32

And be kind to one another, tenderhearted, forgiving one another, even as God in Christ forgave you.

In the blink of an eye, everything can change. So forgive often and love with all of your heart. You may never know when you might have that chance again. - *Unknown*

O n June 26, 1994, at the age of 17, I was shot. The bullet went in through the front of my neck, lodged inside of my spinal cord, instantly leaving me paralyzed from my chest down to my feet.

Just a little over two months prior to June 26, on April 14, 1994, I became a father to twin daughters, Marilyn and Madelyn. I was at their mother's house, visiting them before going home. As I was leaving, I was walking out from between two trailers when a man I will call Charles was running from around the front of one trailer. We accidentally bumped into one another and his hat fell off his head; he was wearing a white University of Alabama hat. When I bent down to pick up his hat, he mouthed off at me and said, "You better pick up my hat."

During that time in my life, I was a hot-headed 17-year-old kid, so I thought someone mouthing off at me was a big deal and needed to be challenged. I stood up with his hat in my hand and we began to argue. He kept saying, "Give me my hat" and I said, "I'm not giving you anything" and I left with his hat in my hand.

I was riding with a man I will call Earl, we were leaving the area. Charles, the man whose hat I knocked off and another man I will call Lester, were following our car on bicycles. Earl asked if I wanted to stop down the road in the dark and mess them up. I replied, "No, I just had twin daughters and I don't need to get into any trouble."

Earl and I went over to a friend's house I will call James and we sat around with him for a while. We all decided that we would try to get to the store before midnight to purchase some beer. It was a Saturday turning into a Sunday, and after midnight, alcohol could not be purchased in Marion, Alabama. Neither of us was old enough to buy beer, but we all looked older than we really were so purchasing beer was not difficult. We did not make it to the store before midnight and were unable to buy the beer.

We then went to a bootlegger's house to buy the beer. We had to drive down a one way street to leave the bootlegger's house. We made a left turn, and a car was coming over the hill behind us flashing their headlights as if they were trying to get us to pull over and stop. We all assumed it was the police, so we pulled over. We had no idea that it was the two men who were following us on bicycles a little over an hour ago. They had found a car and tracked us down.

They pulled over and blocked us in. Earl, the driver of the car I was in, got out. When he did, Charles, the man whose hat I had knocked off, jumped out of the passenger side of the other car, pulled a gun on Earl and threatened to kill him. Charles ran around to the passenger side of the car where I was, pointed the gun at me and threatened to kill me while screaming, "Give me my hat!" I got out of the car and James, the friend we picked up, got out of the car also. Charles was unaware that James was in the back seat. Charles was standing between the two of us and he was not sure who to hold the gun on. Charles panicked and ran back to the car he was in and they sped off.

At that time, I was overtaken by rage and the only thing I could think was that I wanted to catch them and kill one of them with my bare hands. I jumped in the car and screamed; "Go after them!" so Earl went after them.

They made a right turn, went down and turned left into an apartment complex parking lot. I knew that the driver of the car (Lester) had an aunt who lived in that apartment complex. Charles and Lester were sitting in the car, thinking about whether they were going to get out of the car or come back out of the parking lot.

We stopped at the entrance of the parking lot. I got out of our car and stood outside of the car with one foot in and one foot out looking over the top of the car to see if they were going to get out. If they had gotten out, I was going to run down the side of the apartment building and catch one of them. Rage had completely taken over me and I felt as if I could kill one of them with my bare hands. Instead of getting out of the car, they slowly began to pull out of the parking lot. They got to the exit and made a left turn; we were facing the passenger side of the car. As they were making the left turn, Charles shot at me twice, and I literally felt one of the bullets pass my ear.

They sped off, and still enraged, I jumped in the car and screamed again; "Go after them!" They drove away and made a right turn into a horse-shoe-like road. We went to the other end of the horse-shoe-like road and pulled into a driveway on the left side of the road. We got out of the car watching and waiting to see what they were doing. They were slowly driving around; they sped out, made a right turn and came to a complete stop in front of us.

At that time, we were facing the driver's side of their car; Charles reached across Lester from the passenger's side of the car with the gun in his left hand, and shot once. The bullet went in through the front of my neck right below my chin, lodged inside of my spinal cord and left me instantly paralyzed.

The entire time, Charles and I never lost eye contact. As they were speeding away, Charles and I were still looking into each other's eyes until they were out of sight. It was as if time slowed down. Once they were out of sight, time sped up again.

Earl and James ran over to me and asked, "Are you okay?" I replied, "I'm shot." I was still able to talk, but I could not move anything. Earl asked James to grab my legs and help put me in the car, and James said, "No, let's leave him." Earl said, "No, grab his legs." James said, "No, let's leave him. The police are going to think we did it." Earl screamed, "Please grab his legs and help put him in the car; we can't leave him!" Finally, Earl won the argument and James grabbed my legs and they put me in the car; blood was everywhere.

As we were leaving, Earl asked me if I wanted to go to the police station or the hospital. I said, "Take me to the hospital." On our way to the hospital, my body was in so much pain, I felt like I was tied up in knots. I asked Earl if he could stop and straighten out my body because I was hurting so bad. Earl pulled over and as he was walking around the front of the car to come help me, James screamed, "Get in the car they are coming, they are coming to kill us!" Earl ran back around to the driver's side, jumped in the car and attempted to speed off, but the car was a stick shift and it would not go into gear. The car was jerking, it finally went into gear and we sped away.

Lester and Charles were chasing and shooting at us; we were in a high-speed chase. They followed us all the way to the hospital; they were going to kill us to keep us from telling anyone about what happened.

Finally, we made it to the hospital and had to make a sharp right turn at a very high speed. The car should have flipped three or four times, but God kept the tires on the ground. Lester and Charles kept going straight. We went around to the emergency room entrance. Earl pulled me out of the car, laid me on the ground and rang the emergency room bell. James went into my pocket, took my wallet and ran away. The hospital staff came out, placed me on a stretcher and rushed me in. The last thing I remembered was telling the nurse that I could not breathe. She placed an oxygen mask on my face and I became unconscious.

Awaking for the First Time after Becoming Unconscious

I vaguely remember becoming conscious while being rushed through doors. When I became completely conscious, I woke up in the University of Alabama at Birmingham Hospital surrounded by doctors and nurses, attached to monitors, with tubes stuck everywhere inside of me. I had a tracheostomy and a breathing tube attached to a ventilator that was breathing for me; keeping me alive.

When I looked up, the doctor was standing directly over me looking down into my eyes. He asked, "Do you know what's wrong with you?" Because of the tracheostomy I could not talk, so I moved my lips and replied, "Yes," He asked, "What?" I said, "I have been shot." He said, "Yeah, yeah I know that, but do you know what's wrong with you?" I asked, "What?" He said, "You're paralyzed." I replied, "Paralyzed!!!" I asked, "For how long?" He said, "I am afraid you're going to be paralyzed for the rest of your life. You will never walk again, talk again, move again or have any quality of life. You will be a vegetable for the rest of your life." WOW! That was extremely difficult news to wake up to.

He then left my bedside and went to the waiting room where my family was and told them what he had just told me. He recommended that it would be best to pull the plug on my life because it would not be fair to let me live with paralysis. My mother immediately said "No, I am not pulling the plug on my son even if he does have to live with paralysis." My dad disagreed and thought it was best to pull the plug. Thank God for my mother's love.

Threats Being Made on My Life

While I was in the hospital recovering, threats were being made on my life. I do not know if it was Lester and Charles who were behind the threats or if it was someone else. The hospital placed me under different aliases and moved me to different rooms because someone was constantly calling asking for me and saying that they were going to search the entire hospital until they found and killed me. That made my recovery process even more difficult.

My Time in the Hospital and Rehab

I spent approximately five months in the hospital and rehab. I was unable to eat solid foods, so I was fed through a tube. I was on all types of medications; so many I cannot name. I lost my physical ability to do anything for myself. Someone else turned me from side-to-side every two hours, gave me a bath, brushed my teeth, combed my hair, put my clothes on and assisted me in using the bathroom. I had to have an indwelling catheter to urinate and use suppositories every other night for bowel movements. I had to be physically lifted into a wheelchair to move around and wear therapeutic splints on my hands, arms, legs and feet. I weighed 198 pounds before being shot, I lost 118 pounds; I weighed only 80 pounds. I remember looking in the mirror for the first time, I was so skinny and weak looking, all I could do was cry.

Someone made a video of my twin daughters playing and laughing with each other on the couch. The video was only five minutes long, but I watched that video over and over; maybe 100 times a day. That video of my twin daughters brought me so much joy amidst all the pain. The sound of their laughter gave me strength and motivated me to recover; they kept me alive.

My body began to become stronger and I was able to gradually eat solid foods and sit up longer periods of time in my wheelchair. I was gradually weaned off the ventilator as my lungs got stronger. They would cap off the trach tube while I was off the ventilator for a couple hours a day; when the trach tube was capped, I could talk.

Finding out One of My Twin Daughters Died

Whenever the trach tube was capped off, the first thing I would do is call to check on Marilyn and Madelyn. One night I called and the cousin of my daughters' mother answered the telephone; I asked about Madelyn and Marilyn. Then she said, "Why do you keep asking about Madelyn; she is dead. You have to accept it and let it go." I replied, "What do you mean she is dead?" There was a moment of silence. Then I asked again, "What do you mean?" She replied, "Oh my God you did not know! Madelyn died."

That is when I found out that two months after I was shot Madelyn died at four-months-old from sudden infant death syndrome. She had been dead for four months; they had already had her funeral and I never knew anything about it. The doctors had instructed my family not to tell me as they felt it was best, considering all that was taking place in my life at the time. Hearing this news really hit me hard. All I could do was scream, I tried to get up but I could not move anything; my heart felt as if it was going to explode. I was making significant physical improvements; getting that news really set me back.

I was infuriated!!! I was angry with God; I wanted to know how a loving Father could let that happen. I was angry with my family, friends and the mother of my daughters. "Why didn't anyone tell me?" I was angry with Lester and Charles. I thought, "You are going to pay for doing that. Had you not shot me, I would have been there." I was angry with myself. "Why did I not just give him that stupid hat back? This is my entire fault. I would have been there if only I would have just given him that stupid hat." Losing Madelyn was difficult to accept, and the bitterness really set in. I felt like the entire world needed to pay.

Discharged to go Home

A month later, in November, I was discharged. When I came home, there was no one who could properly care for me. My mother was a drug addict and alcoholic, and my father was not in my life. My other family members did not seem to care and no friends came to my aid. Home health workers came out a couple hours a day, but the extent of my care required much more. It was a 24 hour, 7 days-a-week job to care for me.

There was no running water, no heat, and no working appliances; there was only electricity. It was cold in November of that year so my mother hung a blanket over my bedroom door and plugged up a single-eye hot plate to serve as a heater to keep my room warm. We also cooked on that single-eye hot plate. During that time, certain things that were used to care for me such as catheters had to be sterilized, so we also used it for that purpose. We carried buckets of water from the neighbor's house to use for drinking, cooking, bathing and other things.

My body was cold all the time and I also would sweat a lot, so the clammy skin made me feel even colder. I was under an electric blanket all of the time trying to keep warm. Because I could not feel, the electric blanket burnt my legs. That caused even more problems because the burns had to be treated.

My 13-year-old brother was my primary caregiver. He would get up before school to feed me, bathe me and give me my other care. He rushed home after school to care for me even more, and some days he never went to school because he was up all night caring for me. The situation was really bad and it became even worse.

I received my first disability check and used it to buy a large amount of crack cocaine to sell. My intentions were to earn some money to get the utilities turned on and buy some working appliances. I taught my 13-year-old brother how to cut up the crack cocaine and sell it. The situation was really dangerous; a 13-year-old kid and an 18-year-old teenager that was paralyzed from his chest down trying to sell drugs. Eventually someone was going to come in, overpower us and possibly kill us.

My First Opportunity for Revenge

Charles, the man who shot me, only lived about 60 yards from the front of my house. I could look out of my window and see his house. I was obsessed with watching his house; I would get up in my wheelchair and sit at the window for hours watching his house. I knew everything that took place at his house, I could tell you who came to visit, how many times he, his sister, mother and father went in and out of the house, what they were wearing, what time they left and returned. I wanted revenge!

Charles had a very loud sound system inside of his car and he would ride past my house multiple times throughout the day playing his music so loud that it would vibrate the pictures on my wall. Every time he passed my house, he would always play the same song, "Murder was the Case" by Snoop Dog. It was as if he was flaunting what he had done in my face.

One night a guy came to my house and told me if I gave him a certain amount of crack cocaine that he would kill Charles and his family for me. I asked him, "How will I know you did it?" He said, "You can look out of the window and watch the house go up in flames. I'm going to burn the house down while they are asleep."

I had the amount of drugs that he wanted. I was angry, bitter, and wanted revenge. I thought about what Charles had done to me. I thought about my daughter dying, and how he was free on the streets, riding past my house and flaunting his freedom. My reason for killing him and his family was justified, but for whatever reason, I told the guy no.

The guy fell on his knees, took my hand and said, "Look at what he has done to you; he deserves it. Please give me the drugs and I will kill them for you and you can watch me do it." With tears rolling down my face and my heart beating rapidly, I said, "No." I had an opportunity to have a front row seat and watch the person who caused me so much pain die and I said, "No." I cannot explain why I said no because Christ was not in my heart at that time in my life and every part of my being wanted revenge. All I can say is that I am so glad that I said no.

A THOUGHT TO TAKE

100% of the time an emotional decision is a bad decision. No matter how justified the desire for revenge is or how enraged you are, it is wrong. Acting in rage or pursuing revenge will only lead to more destruction and pain in your life and the lives of others.

Chapter 2

Going to the Nursing Home

....

Mark 11:25

And whenever you stand praying, if you have anything against anyone, forgive him, that your Father in heaven may also forgive you your trespasses.

Forgiveness is a gift. You must find a way to forgive regardless of what or who has dropped you into a grievous state of affairs. Forgiveness leads to your freedom. - Unknown

The situation at home was too bad for me to continue to live there in my condition. I was paralyzed from my chest down, there was no one to care properly for me, and my 13-year-old brother and I were trying to sell drugs to survive. We both were going to be killed or I was going to die from a lack of proper care.

One day I called my brother in the room, explained to him how terrible of a situation we were in and told him I needed him to walk down the road to the telephone booth and call the Department of Human Resources (DHR) and ask them to come get me out of our home. My little brother could not understand why I needed to do it. He asked me, "But if you leave, who will be here with me; who will I have?" He was all I had and I was all he had. I explained to him that if I did not leave, I was going to die or someone was going to come in and kill us. He understood and walked to the telephone booth and called DHR. That must have been the longest walk of his life and a difficult thing for a 13-year-old kid to do. As difficult as it was, making the call was the right thing to do; it saved both of us.

Less than an hour after my brother made the call to DHR the house was surrounded with police and an ambulance to take me out of the home. No one but my brother and I knew that DHR was coming. When they came in to get me, my mother was fighting with them, trying to get them to leave me alone and let me stay. I then told my mother I had called DHR to come because if I stayed I was going to die. It was a hard thing for my mother to hear me say and very painful for her to helplessly sit by and watch her child being taken out of her home and not be able to do anything to stop it.

The paramedics placed me on the stretcher, loaded me inside the ambulance and took me to a hospital in Selma Alabama where I was admitted from February 14, 1995 to March 15, 1995. The very next day, to my surprise, my father came to visit me. I had not seen him since I left the hospital in Birmingham. He visited me every single day while I was there. (I will share more about my father in Chapter Four.)

Life in the Nursing Home Begins

On March 15, 1995, I was transferred to a nursing home in Tuskegee, Alabama. I always thought a person had to be in their old age before going to a nursing home, but there I was, 18-years-old in a nursing home. Most 18-year-olds were graduating high school, going to the prom, preparing for college etc.; doing all of the normal things 18-year-olds do.

And there I was, surrounded by elderly people who were in the senile stages of life. I would constantly hear them screaming, "I want my momma", would awaken to the smell of feces and urine every single day, surrounded by death as someone died every day, and I was being abused and neglected.

I was hundreds of miles from home, surrounded by strangers and unfamiliar things, and my family had abandoned me. Everyone knows that a nursing home is a last resort; it is the place that you send people to spend the remainder of their days. No one cared enough to take the time to seek other available options; they just simply gave up on me before giving me a chance and placed me there to die.

I was in two different nursing homes for a total of 2 years, 3 months, and 5 days. During that time, I did not receive a visit from a family member or loved one, and I was abused and neglected. Even the details that I am sharing with you cannot begin to scratch the surface of the abuse and neglect that happens in nursing homes, especially to those people who are there without family around and are unable to verbally express what is being done to them.

What do you do when you are 18-years-old in a nursing home, lying flat on your back paralyzed from your chest down, in a town that is hundreds of miles away from anyone or anything you know and everyone who should be there for you is not there? I did not know what to do and my anger grew; I was mad at the world.

I was angry, depressed and felt hopeless. I did not want to eat; I did not want to get out of the bed; I did not want anyone to come in my room; I did not want anyone to turn on the lights or open the shades. I just wanted to be left alone to die.

Day after day, I would lie there replaying the details of June 26, 1994 over and over in my mind. I could not stop thinking about Lester and Charles. How unfair it was for me to be there, locked up in the nursing home like I was the criminal and they were out; freely enjoying their lives. They had taken away my ability to walk and move; they had taken me away from my daughter; I was unable to see or hold her. They had taken my life. I blamed them for every painful and wrong thing in my life and the more I thought about them, the bitterer I became.

The Abuse and Neglect

To this day, my arms are contracted; I cannot fully extend them because of the abuse I received in the nursing home. There were days when I would lie in soiled sheets with feces and urine for upward of twelve hours, and because I was not being turned every two hours, I began to develop pressure sores on my behind, legs and feet. These health issues came from a lack of proper care; it made my condition even worse.

I recall one day I had not had a bath all day. Baths were given on the first shift, so if I did not get a bath on the first shift, there was no way anyone on the second or third shift was going to do it; I would have to wait until the next day. I began to press the call light and ask if I could have a bath. They would answer and say that someone would be with me shortly, but hours would pass and no one came. It was about 30 minutes before the end of the first shift and I knew that if I did not get a bath then, I would have to wait until the next day so I pressed the call light again and asked for a bath. When I did, the nursing assistant caring for me stormed in the room screaming and cursing. He grabbed a pillow and was about to place it over my face to smother me when another nursing assistant walked in the room. He then pretended he was placing the pillow under my head; he even fluffed the pillow and asked if I was comfortable, all while smiling when the other assistant was looking.

My roommate was an older man; with both of his legs amputated. He had sores on his behind so big that you could stick your fist inside of them. I have seen workers hold feces on a spoon to a senile man's mouth to see if he would eat it, and watched workers making the older people fight with one another. All of it was entertainment for them. I have witnessed unsupervised patients roll down stairs and break their necks and die, and the nursing home simply covered it up.

I attempted to report the abuse and neglect that was being done to all of us, but it only made life worse for me. The nurses and assistants would not talk to me, and whenever they would come in my room, it was always two or more at a time so I felt like I was being teamed up on. When they were bathing me or turning me, it was done with force. There was absolutely nothing that I could do, but take it. The mistreatment pushed me into a deeper depression and increased my bitterness.

All the staff knew I had no family seeing about me; so who was I going to tell? Without family or loved ones on the outside fighting for your rights, you were simply nobody in that nursing home. The administration, social workers, patient care advocates and state Ombudsman who were supposed to be fighting for the patients' rights, did not do anything to protect the patients. They were all friends and knew one another and they worked together to cover the abuse and neglect.

As a patient living inside a nursing home, I got firsthand experience of how things were done. The beautiful building with the pretty grass and flowers is what people on the outside see. As a patient on the inside looking out, I saw the abuse, neglect and cover-ups.

When it was time for the annual state inspection, which was an inspection that was marked on the calendar, everything was clean, in order and done to perfection. Meals were on time, baths were given, you were turned every two hours and someone would magically appear by your room just to say hello and see how your day was going. This occurred especially in my room because they wanted to make sure I would not tell anyone what was really going on in there, and if I did tell anyone, they wanted to know about it, so I was watched closely.

I am sure there are good nursing homes that run things decently and in order, provide their patients with the best care possible and work hard to provide an environment that is clean and safe. I am only speaking from my personal experience.

Scared for My Life

One day I was looking through my patient chart and I saw something written in it that had me scared for my life. The physician had written in big black letters **"Lorenzo is mentally unstable, experiencing hallucinations and needs to be medicated."** There was absolutely nothing wrong with me mentally, but they were about to change that by medicating me. They were not going to allow me, a patient that had the mental ability to verbally expose their negligence shut their facility down, they were going to do whatever it took to cover themselves and shut me up.

I knew I was all alone and had no one I could reach out to for help. I was already experiencing the consequences of filing a complaint, but I never in a million years would have thought they would go so far as to medicate me to shut me up. I was scared for my life, so I shut my mouth and never complained again; I just took whatever care was given. There were many days when I was not bathed, I did not get turned, I laid in feces and urine, and my meals were late, but I never said a word. Imagine being in a situation and not having any control over the way other people treat you. It can cause anyone to become resentful.

Years earlier, when I was still at home in that house with no utilities, running water or working appliances, I was reading the Bible and I randomly opened it to *James 1:19-20* *which says, "Understand [this], my beloved brethren. Let* *every man be quick to hear [a ready listener], slow to speak,* *slow to take offense and to get angry. For man's anger does* *not promote the righteousness God [wishes and requires]."* All of sudden one day, this scripture came back to my mind and I began to say it over and over and I found comfort in it. That scripture got me through all of those days I was forced to close my mouth and not say anything because I was scared for my life.

It would not be fair for me to say every worker was terrible and cruel. For every bad person in the world, there are also those who are good. I have to specifically acknowledge Sophia Dowdell, an RN, at the facility. She and her family embraced me and showed me love. They would take me to their home and treat me like family. Sophia would take her own personal income and buy me clothes and shoes. Also, Cortez Drisker, an LPN, who always had a joke and made me laugh on days when I was really down. Rodney Beasley a CPA, who picked me up on his off days and took me to college basketball games. Multiple workers were extremely kind to me. To every worker who treated me with kindness and dignity, your kindnesses toward me will never be forgotten.

God Begins to Move

One day Jackie Spears, the physical therapist, looked at me and said, "You look so sad; how can I help you?" I said, "I need a friend." The next day she introduced me to Latrice Heard, a young lady who later became one of my best friends. Latrice and her husband Chris were very good to me. Latrice would pick me up every weekend and take me to their home, out to the mall or just to ride around. Her friendship was just what I needed. Finally, I had someone who really cared for me, someone who was on the outside who showed their face regularly. I cannot even begin to tell you the impact of having a friend who really cared. Just one person who cared enough to listen to me, cry with me and laugh with me. This world is a really big place and no one should be alone in it. Latrice's friendship gave me a spark of joy and helped ease the bitterness in my heart.

One day I was sitting beside the phone booth at the front door of the nursing home looking out when these two little kids walked in to use the telephone. It was a little girl around 12-years-old and a little boy around 9-years-old. After the girl finished using the telephone she turned to me and asked, "How old are you; you look young?" I answered, "19" She instantly began to minister to me and said; "Don't worry, God is going to work everything out," then they turned and left.

The next day I was sitting in the hallway when those same two kids were walking toward me with an older teenage girl. I remember looking at the older teenage girl walking toward me thinking to myself "That is the most beautiful girl I have ever seen." They walked up to me and the older teenage girl introduced herself and said, "Hey, my name is Shanika Browning and my brother and sister came home yesterday and told me about you and said I needed to come to meet you and we want to know if we can come read the Bible to you and pray with you sometime?"

Prior to that, pastors and people from the church would come to the nursing home, go around to patients rooms, and ask to pray with them and to read the Bible to them. Whenever they would come around to my room, I would scream at them and say, "Get out of my room. I don't want to hear anything about God or the Bible; I don't want anyone praying for me!"

I was bitter and angry with the world and I was especially angry with God.

But, when that teenage girl asked me, I looked up with a smile on my face and said, "Sure, no problem" and to be honest, I really did not want to hear anything about God or the Bible, I just wanted to look at Shanika and that was a way to get her to come visit me.

Little did I know, God was about to use Shanika to change my life and save my soul. Shanika, her brother and sister, Raphel and Lanora would come to the nursing home every day and read the Bible to me. That changed my life and Shanika led me to accept Christ as my Lord and Savior.

The entire Browning family embraced me. Their father, Mr. Melvin Browning, would come to pick me up on Sundays and physically lift me from my wheelchair into his car and take me to church. Their older brother, cousins and grandparents all displayed a level of love toward me that was unexplainable. I could not believe that a group of total strangers could love me like that.

The Browning family loved Christ and it showed through their love and acceptance of me. I was bitter and angry with the entire world; I wanted everyone to suffer just as I was suffering and my heart was hard and filled with hatred. The love I received from the Browning family helped restore my faith in humanity. They showed me there were people out there who cared. Their love toward me permitted me to trust people again and opened my heart to love again.

A group of nursing students from a local college were at the nursing home doing their clinicals. The majority of the students was my age and amazed that a guy their age was in the nursing home and it created a buzz amongst the students.

Their nursing instructor, Mrs. Beatrice Morgan, wanted to know what the talk was all about and came to my room. When she saw me she said, "Oh now I see" then she asked me, "What are you doing here?" I replied, "I was shot." She said, "No, why are you here?" I said, "DHR placed me here." She said, "No, where is your family?" I replied, "My family is unable to care for me." Then she asked me a question that would forever change my life. She asked, "Well, what are you going to do?" I asked, "What do you mean?" She said, "Well you do want to get out of here, don't you?" Well, prior to that moment, it had never crossed my mind that I could ever leave there. I answered and said, "Yeah, I guess I do." She said, "Well, let me think about a few things and get back with you."

The next day, Mrs. Morgan came back and asked if I would be interested in doing public speaking. She arranged for the Opelika-Auburn News to come out and do an article about me. On the front page of their newspaper was a picture of me and under it the article said, "Nineteen-year-old in a nursing home was shot and left paralyzed from his chest down. He would like to tell his story and help others." From that point, the calls started coming in and I began speaking at schools, churches, programs and events. Using my pain, mistakes and experiences to help others, in my opinion, helped me more than it helped them.

Mrs. Beatrice Morgan made me believe in myself. She helped me discover strengths inside of me I never knew existed. She helped me get off my soapbox and stop blaming others for everything wrong and painful in my life and start taking matters into my own hands. She opened my eyes to see that my life was not over just because I was paralyzed or living in a nursing home. She led me to discover my purpose in life.

The Speaking Engagement that Changed my Life

I was invited to speak at Tuskegee University to a group of occupational therapy students. One of the students did an internship at an organization called Alabama Department of Rehabilitation Services (ADRS). I had never heard of that organization before that day. The student connected me with the organization and they began to work with me.

They sent a worker out to see me name Patti Nelson. Patti was a God-send; she went above and beyond the call of duty and stood toe-to-toe with the nursing home and DHR. She fought for my right to live outside of a nursing home. She opened doors for me through ADRS that led to getting out of the nursing home, receiving my very first electric wheelchair and getting the rehabilitation needed to live on my own again.

The Reason I was Able to Forgive

I knew who Christ was, because my mother and grandmother talked about Him often and the church bus picked us up every Sunday when I was a kid. But I had never experienced the depths of His magnificent, unmatchable and unconditional love this way before. His love had captured me and for the first time I realized why He suffered and died for me. I had been forgiven and I did not do anything to earn it or deserve it. I wanted others to experience the depths of His love and I wanted everyone to experience it through my forgiveness toward them.

A THOUGHT TO TAKE

God knows what we need, when we need it and what it takes to get it to us. He is acquainted with all of our ways. There is nowhere we can go from His Spirit and nowhere can we flee from His presence. He will reach out to you and meet you right where you are and provide you with everything that you need to forgive and live again.

Chapter 3

Forgiving the Men Who Left Me Paralyzed

....

Matthew 6:15

But if you do not forgive men their trespasses, neither will your Father forgive your trespasses.

To forgive is to set a prisoner free only to discover that the prisoner was you - Lewis B. Smedes

Forgiving a stranger is less difficult than forgiving someone you know. When someone you know offends you, it hurts deep on the inside; you are dealing with matters of the heart.

I grew up with both Lester and Charles; I knew their parents, siblings and all of their extended family members. Lester and I were childhood best friends; we played together every day and stayed over each other's houses nearly every weekend. Lester, Charles and I had been in the exact same classroom with one another since Pre-K. We saw each other nearly every day of our lives. We ate lunch together, played basketball together and hung out together; we were friends. To be offended by them did not just hurt me physically, but it really hurt me emotionally; deep down on the inside.

One Week Before the Shooting

I was working at a local restaurant and had opened a savings account at the local bank where Charles's mother worked as a teller. A week before the shooting, Me, Charles, and some other guys were hanging out talking. Charles turned to me and said, "You won't believe what my mother said to me last night. She said I need to be more like Mattie Brown's son and I asked; are you talking about Lorenzo Brown? Can you believe my mother said that to me?" and we all laughed about it.

It was funny his mother said that to him, because I was not living a lifestyle that would exemplify a role model. But when my twin daughters were born, I had begun to make a turn for the better and Charles's mother recognized it. I believe the words Charles's mother spoke to him that night touched him in the wrong way and caused him to harbor secret anger and resentment in his heart toward me. On the night he and I bumped into one another and his hat fell off his head, an opportunity clashed with the secret anger and resentment in his heart, and it gave him a reason to act upon it.

Trial Time

On June 27, 1994, the very next day after the shooting, Lester and Charles were both picked up by the police and placed in jail. Two weeks later, they both made bond and were released. Two years later, in the summer of 1996, we went to trial. The trial was a joke from the beginning. First of all, I was appointed a young attorney to handle my case; I was not sure if he had any courtroom experience. Secondly, Earl who was the driver of the car I was in the night of the shooting was supposed to be a witness on my behalf, never showed up for court. James, who was also in the car with me the night of the shooting was supposed to be a witness on my behalf, showed up for court, but told my attorney that he would only testify if he were paid. Thirdly, Lester never showed up for court. Charles was equipped with a high profile expensive attorney whom my young court-appointed attorney was in awe over. I heard my attorney say that Charles's attorney was his mentor. He absolutely could not believe that he was presenting a case opposite of Charles's attorney. His eyes gleamed like a little kid every time Charles's attorney spoke.

Charles's attorney questioned me and asked, "In what month and on what day did the shooting take place?" I responded, "On June 26, 1994." He then presented some pictures of the location where the shooting happened and asked, "Is this the location where you supposedly were shot?" I replied, "Yes" He then asked, "Are there any leaves on the trees in these pictures?" I answered, "No," then he asked, "Should any leaves be on trees in the month of June?" I answered, "Yes," He then said, "Well if leaves are supposed to be on the trees in the month of June and there are none there in the pictures then it is apparent that you are not even sure about when you were supposedly shot." He took pictures of the scene during a winter month and presented them. What leaves being on trees had to do with my case I am not sure but what baffled my mind is that my attorney never bothered to present any police records to confirm I was telling the truth.

Charles was questioned by his attorney and was asked, "Have you ever shot a gun before?" Charles replied, "No, I have never seen a real gun unless it was in a magazine or a school book." His attorney asked, "If you have never seen a real gun before then who shot Mr. Brown?" Charles answered, "I do not know" and even though Lester and Earl were subpoenaed to come to court, they did not show up and were not picked up to testify and James was not questioned even though he was there.

All twelve jurors went back to deliberate. Eleven jurors entered a guilty verdict and one juror was undecided. The judge postponed the decision for two days to give jurors time to decide. Everyone was asked to return to court after two days. When it was time to return I did not come back. When I did not come back, it was ruled either a hung jury or thrown out of court.

Why I Didn't Return

During the time of the trial, I was staying in the nursing home in Tuskegee, Alabama, hundreds of miles away from Marion, Alabama, where the trial was held. Traveling for me during the early stages of my paralysis was difficult. Sitting up in my wheelchair during the two and-a-half hour, one-way trip was very painful. I had to be loaded inside the van and driven from Tuskegee to Marion for court and back to Tuskegee after court. The drive time alone was five hours; when you include the time we spent in court, my body was in terrible pain.

During those two days, while waiting to return to court, I did not get one second of sleep. I stayed up, replaying over-and-over in my mind every detail of the night of June 26, 1994. I counted the years, months, days, hours, minutes, and seconds of how long I had been paralyzed. I was so tense that I had literally chewed a hole in my pinky finger while thinking about all of it and I was not aware I had done it.

I had finally accepted the fact that I was paralyzed and would possibly never walk again. I had accepted Christ as my Lord and Savior and He had healed my heart from all of the hatred and anger that I was once living with and now because of this trial I was reliving it all over again

I could feel the anger returning. All I could think about was Charles lying on the stand about not seeing a real gun and saying he did not shoot me. I thought about how the justice system of Marion, Alabama had failed me by appointing me an inexperienced young attorney. I thought about how no one was sent to pick up Lester or Earl, to make them take the stand, and how James was never questioned. It was as if it was all just a big joke, just a formality. I felt like I was a nobody!

The desire for revenge filled me once again; I then thought to myself how I wish I had given that guy the drugs when I had the chance and let him kill Charles and his family. I could not stop crying and my head was hurting so bad and I was so angry; I felt like I was going to explode.

Shanika went to court with me. Afterwards, she and I prayed and read scriptures about forgiveness. During our time of prayer and reading scriptures, I felt a peace come over me; a peace that surpassed all understanding. All of the anger, bitterness, resentment, and desire for revenge that had returned left me and I came to the conclusion within myself that I was at peace about whatever the jurors decided.

On the morning when it was time to return to court, the social worker came to my room to get me and I told her I was not going back. She asked, "Why?" I told her, "I cannot relive this all over again." She understood and no one pressured me to return. Later that day, the social worker returned to my room to inform me of the jurors' decision. Initially, I was very hurt and disappointed to hear that no one would serve any prison time for shooting me. All I could do was cry. After a few weeks, I accepted things for the way they were and I was free.

Face-to-Face Forgiveness

During Christmas of 1998, I returned to my hometown for the first time since the trial. A little over two years had passed and a lot had taken place in my life but one of the most liberating things I had ever done was about to take place. I knew once I was in Marion, Alabama there would be a possibility that I would see Lester and Charles. I was not sure how I would react if I did see them face-to-face for the first time. Just as I assumed, when I got out of the van, I saw Lester walking out of his aunt's house. I had not planned to do it, but I called to him and when he turned around and saw me, his face looked like he had seen a ghost. I called him over and I looked him directly in his eyes and said, "I want you to know that I love you and I forgive you" then I gave him a hug.

In the summer of 1999, I returned to my hometown, and as we were getting gas, to my surprise, Charles walked out of the gas station. It had been over three years since I had seen Charles and one of the last images I had of him was when he took the stand in the courtroom. When he walked out of the gas station, that image flashed through my mind. And the words he spoke on the stand, "I have never seen a real gun before; the only time I have ever seen a gun was in a magazine or school book; I do not know who shot Mr. Brown" were loud and clear in my mind. I called for Charles and he was just as surprised to see me. He came over to the car and I asked him to open the door; he opened the door and sat down. We had a brief conversation then I looked him directly in his eyes and said, "I want you to know that I love you and forgive you," then I gave him a hug; just as I did with Lester.

I had already forgiven Lester and Charles in my heart, but I never knew the day would come that I would come face-to-face with them again. It was not something I had planned; I had never given any thought about seeing either one of them again. It was all a part of God's plan; a plan to set me free to live. Although Lester and Charles did not receive a guilty verdict from the justice system, when I looked them in their eyes and said, "I love you and I forgive you," it set them free to live in a way that no justice system ever could. Only the love of Christ can set both the offender and the one that has been offended free at the same time.

A Moment that Touched My Heart

In 2010 my wife, twin sons and I were picking my daughter up from Marion to come to Birmingham with us for the summer. While we were sitting in the parking lot waiting on her to come out, Lester walked over to the van. I rolled the window down and I introduced him to my family. He and I began to have a conversation and he shared with me that things were not going good in his life and he really needed to get some things together. Then he asked me, if I would pray for him; that really touched my heart. Lester was partly responsible for my paralysis and he caused a lot of pain in my life but because I extended total forgiveness toward him, he believed in his heart that I cared enough for him to pray for him. I did care and I prayed for him at that very moment. After we finished praying, he looked me in my eyes and said, "I love you." I cannot even explain how moving of a moment it was. In 1998, I looked him in his eyes and said, "I love you and I forgive you" and now because of my forgiveness and love to him; he is able to look me in my eyes and do the same. Forgiveness is pleasing unto the Lord and when a man's ways please the Lord, he makes even his enemies to be at peace with him (Proverbs 16:7).

A Purpose Greater than Myself

In September of 2008, I was invited to my hometown high school to speak to the 8th – 12th grade male students. The principal wanted the male students to get their year started on the right foot so they invited me to inspire them.

I spoke at two different sessions; in the second session, Charles's son was in the audience. I shared a brief portion of how I became paralyzed, but, as I was speaking, Charles's son never knew I was talking about his father. Afterwards, I told the students I would stay around if any of them needed me to pray or to talk with them about anything. Three of the male students stayed and Charles's son was one of them. He walked up to me and introduced himself; he has the same name as his father. He asked me if I knew his father; I replied, "Yes I know your father, I went to school with him and played basketball with him" then I asked, "How can I help you?" His reply rocked my world. He said, "Last year I did something to one of the teachers and I have been struggling with unforgiveness; can you tell me how to forgive?" I told him how to forgive and prayed with him. Then he walked over to the teacher and from a distance I could see them hugging and crying. The teacher was the same one who invited me to speak to the students. When I saw them hugging and crying, I started crying also. I was crying because 14 years prior, his father shot me and left me paralyzed from my chest down to my feet. He never received any prison time and he never apologized to me for what he had done. God used me to lead the son of the man who shot me to forgiveness.

If I had one ounce of unforgiveness in my heart, God would not have been able to use me for His purpose in that moment. When a person has any hatred, bitterness or resentment in their heart toward someone who has hurt them, they do not just want the person who hurt them to suffer; they want everyone that is connected to that person to suffer. There would not have been a better opportunity than that moment to inflict pain back on Charles by hurting his son, but because my heart was 100% free of any hatred, bitterness or resentment, God was able to use me for a purpose that was greater than me. Forgiveness is not for the other person; forgiveness is for you. God will always use a vessel that forgives for a purpose that is greater than them.

The Magnificent Benefits of Forgiveness

In January of 2009, my daughter was playing on the girls' basketball team and they were playing their rival team. In Marion, Alabama whenever rival teams compete, everyone in town comes out. We drove down from Birmingham to watch my daughter play; I was sitting at the front by the door. When I looked up, Charles, his wife and children were walking in the gym; they walked by me and did not see me. The home side of the gym was full so they had to walk around and sit on the visitors' side; I was watching them the entire time. Their next-to-the-oldest son was sitting three people down from me and Charles's wife was looking around the gym for him, and when she saw him, she looked over and saw me. When she saw me she nudged Charles with her elbow and told him that I was in the gym. Charles looked at me and our eyes locked; he nodded his head and I nodded back and we went on to watch the game.

As we were watching the game, I looked over at Charles with his wife and five children and the Holy Spirit began to move inside of me; I was so overwhelmed by the Spirit that I was in tears. The Father showed me that if I had returned to court that day instead of letting it go, Charles would have been in prison and, with the exception of his oldest son, four of his children would not have life today. Because of my forgiveness toward him, he was able to have a life free of prison and give life to four more children. Only an all-knowing, all-loving Heavenly Father could look out into the future and see the magnificent benefits that a simple thing like forgiveness can bring

My Daughter Saves Charles's Son's Life

My daughter has always known about the person who shot me. She was in school with his son and shared classes with him. I told her I did not want her to ever say anything mean to his son or mistreat him in any way because of something his father had done. And she never did say a mean word to him or mistreat him in any way.

During spring break of 2009, my daughter and I were sitting at the kitchen table talking and she said, "Dad I need to ask you something. Charles's son would like to date me; how would you feel about that?" I asked, "Do you like him?" She replied, "Kind of; sort of." I said, "Well I'm not sure if it would be wise for you to date him; however you can be friends with him." She went on to become friends with Charles's son.

A couple weeks after my daughter returned home from spring break, she called me and said, "Dad I got a call about 2:00 am and it was Charles's son. He said, "I just called to tell you goodbye one last time because I am going to kill myself." My daughter prayed with him and talked him out of committing suicide. She saved the life of the son of the man who shot me.

The reason why God was able to use my daughter to save Charles's son's life was because she watched me walk in love and forgiveness toward Charles. Charles caused a lot of pain in my life, but my daughter saw her father forgive the man who caused him pain and it resulted in her having a forgiving heart. Your children will learn from you. If you are walking in unforgiveness toward someone who has offended you in any way and you display the anger, bitterness and resentment you have for that person in front of your children, they will learn from you and walk in unforgiveness toward the person who offends them. But if they see you forgive and walk in love toward the person who offended you, when they are offended by someone in life, they will learn from you and walk in forgiveness and love toward the person who offends them.

A Hug Says Everything

In August of 2013, I was invited to speak at a youth program in my hometown. Charles's mother and sister were in the audience. His mother sat on the front row and never looked over to acknowledge me at any time during the program. Two speakers and a youth dance group were before me on the program. As I was being introduced, I looked over at Charles's mother and I could see her physically shaking and breathing hard. She got up, walked back to the fourth row where her daughter was sitting, whispered in her ear and they both left the building. Each speaker was given 20 minutes to speak. At the end of my 20 minutes, I was asked to speak an additional five minutes to expound on some things. Charles's mother and sister came back in about two minutes before I finished speaking. I am not sure if they intentionally stayed out until my 20 minutes were over or not; but I do know that God intentionally allowed me five additional minutes.

Charles's mother sat back down on the front row in front of me. After I finished speaking, I went directly to her and put my arms around her. She asked me, "Do you remember me?" I answered, "Yes ma'am, I do remember you." Then I returned to where I was sitting. The last time I saw Charles's mother was in the courtroom when she was standing beside her son with her arms around him defending his innocence when they both knew he was guilty. So when she asked, "Do you remember me?" What she was really asking was, "Do you know who you are hugging?" When I replied, "Yes ma'am, I do remember you." What I was really saying was, "I know that I am hugging the mother of the man who shot me."

If you are holding hatred in your heart toward someone who has offended you and you think you can never let it go unless they apologize, acknowledge that they were wrong, or until justice is done; you will never be free. Your unwillingness to forgive will keep you in bondage. Without forgiveness, there is only anger, bitterness and resentment; but no closure. Forgiveness sets you free to live.

A THOUGHT TO TAKE

An apology is not necessary in order for you to forgive. You have to be at peace with yourself and accept things for the way that they are. Forgive them; even if they don't apologize.

Chapter 4

Forgiving My Parents

Luke 6:37

Judge not, and you shall not be judged. Condemn not, and you shall not be condemned. Forgive, and you will be forgiven.

Forgiveness is the best form of love. It takes a strong person to say they're sorry and an even stronger person to forgive. - *Unknown*

My parents met in high school, fell in love and during a night of teenage passion, they conceived me. Their plan was to get married, spend the rest of their lives together and live happily ever after, but that plan did not happen. Of course, there are two sides to every story, and depending on who is telling the story, my mother or my father, the version is different as to why they broke up and did not get married. Nevertheless, I was conceived and I was caught between battles of two people who were bitter with each other. What a terrible position for a kid to be in.

My mother always had terrible things to say about my father and my father always had terrible things to say about my mother. There was so much anger and bitterness in their hearts for one another. I felt like my mother wanted me to hate my father because she hated him and I felt like my father wanted me to hate my mother because he hated her. I do not know what really happened between my parents and honestly, as a kid I did not care. All I wanted was to love both my mother and father and for them to love each other.

A Lesson for Parents

As a kid, I was always torn between the battles my parents had with one another and I disliked being used as leverage by my parents to hurt one another. An innocent kid should not be caught in the middle of a battle between two bitter adults and should never be forced to choose between which of their parents to love.

If you have conceived a child with someone you once loved but you now hate, you are going to have to find a way to forgive that person. If you cannot forgive them for yourself; then forgive them for the sake of the child. As long as you have a child together, you are always going to be a part of each other's lives even if you are no longer together. Do not let the first lesson that your child receives in unforgiveness come from you.

My Mother's Story

My mother is the oldest girl of six siblings; John, Madelyn (my mother), Lester, Jeffery, David and Claudia. Lester was trapped in a fire that started in the workshop at school and he died because of that fire. I heard stories about my uncle all of the time and the stories were always filled with lots of love and laughter. She loved her brother and had to find a way to live with his death as well as forgive many people who could have been blamed for his death.

When my mother was 24-years-old, her mother died from kidney disease. After her mom died, she was left with the responsibility of caring for Jeffery, David and Claudia. Losing a mother at the age of 24 can have a profound effect on a person. Add to it the responsibility of caring for three younger siblings would have been overwhelming for anyone.

My mother gave birth to two more children, my brothers Alonzo and William so she was a young woman with many responsibilities and life had a different set of plans for her than the plans she had for herself. The death of her brother, the passing of her mother, the responsibilities of her children and her siblings became too much for her to handle and she retreated.

My Mother's Addiction

By the age of 28, my mother had become an alcoholic. I will never forget the night I saw my mother drunk for the first time when I was 10-years-old; it scared the living day lights out of me. I could not believe that was my mother. She was such a beautiful, well-put-together woman. The house was always clean, food was always cooked, and clothes were always clean. She took such great care of our home and us. She was the backbone of our family. My mother graduated to the stronger substance of crack cocaine. The combination of alcohol and crack led to things becoming really bad in all of our lives. It turned our lives upside down.

We moved from house to house; there were times when we did not have food, electricity, heat or running water. The house was not clean anymore, food was not cooked and clothes were not clean. Many days my mother did not even come home; we were left home alone to figure things out for ourselves.

We lived in a small town where everybody knew everybody and my mother was known as one of the town drunks. I cannot explain to you what it was like to be walking through town with my teenage friends seeing my mother standing on the corner begging for money to buy drugs and alcohol. She was willing to sell her body and do other things to get drugs and alcohol. I have dragged my mother out of ditches; I have fought with grown men to keep them from beating and raping her. I got into many fights at school with other kids because they were talking bad about my mother. I hated my mother for everything I had to go through and I lived with a deep hatred in my heart toward her for a long time.

As I explained earlier, after I became paralyzed, my family could not provide me with the care I needed so I was sent to a nursing home. That deepened my hatred for my mother and my family. I was in two different nursing homes for 2 years, 3 months, and 5 days and I never received a visit from my mother or any other member of my family. I knew my mother's addiction was the primary reason for her not being there.

The Lord Sets His Plan in Play for My Mother's Life

Around Christmas of 2000, I went to my hometown to pick my daughter up for the holiday. I went into town before leaving to see my mother and there she was, standing on the same corner doing the same thing. That day something in my heart was different; the hatred, anger, and bitterness I had been carrying in my heart toward my mother for years had suddenly turned to compassion.

I called my mother over to the car; she came running with tears flowing down her face, screaming, "My baby! My baby!" After more than an hour, I finally convinced her to leave Marion, Alabama and come to Birmingham to spend Christmas with us. I had no idea that day would be the last day my mother would ever spend in Marion, standing on the corner. That very moment set the Lord's plan in play for my mother to get off drugs and alcohol and to get her life back.

New Year's Eve of 2000, my mother was headed back to Marion with some other family members when the police stopped them in Bibb County. The police searched the car and found a crack pipe in my mother's purse; she was charged with possession of drug paraphernalia and taken to jail. She stayed in jail for a little over a month before some unknown person paid her bond. To this day, she still does not know who posted her bail.

After being released from jail, instead of going to Marion, to my surprise, she came back to Birmingham. A few days after being back in Birmingham, she started walking the streets looking for drugs and alcohol again. I begged her not to but she continued anyway and her actions caused all of the old feelings I had toward her to resurface.

The Moment I Forgave My Mother

I started to think about all of the things I went through as a kid because of her addiction and I felt the hatred in my heart again. About a week after these old feelings had resurfaced, I was sitting in the park talking to the Lord about my mother. I went on and on telling the Lord about all the things she had done, how she hurt me, and why I hated her. Then as clear as a sunny day, I heard the Lord say to me, "Forgive her." I replied and said, "Lord she doesn't deserve to be forgiven." Then the Lord said, "Son, she may have not earned it, but she does deserve it." That very moment with tears rolling down my face, I forgave my mother for everything and started walking in love toward her.

The Blood of Jesus Cleanses My Mother

A few weeks later, I had some communion juice in the refrigerator; it was in a bottle that looked like a champagne bottle. I noticed my mother had not left home for a few days and I wondered why. When I went to get the communion juice it was gone. I asked my mother what happened to the communion juice. She replied and said, "Boy you know you can't leave any wine in this house around me." I started laughing. She replied, "What are you laughing at? That's the best wine I have ever drunk in my life." She had not left home because she was sneaking and drinking the communion juice that she thought was wine.

Two weeks later on April 23, 2001, my mother stopped drinking alcohol and stopped doing drugs. She thought she was drinking wine but she was really drinking the Blood of Jesus and it washed her white as snow! To this day, my mother is still clean of drugs and alcohol.

If all of the hatred, anger and bitterness I had in my heart toward my mother had not turned to compassion, my mother would not have come to Birmingham with us. Had I not forgave her and began to walk in love toward her; the love of Christ would not have been shown to her. Hatred, anger and bitterness cannot live in the heart of a person who has compassion, walks in love, and extends forgiveness. Miracles happen when forgiveness is given.

My Relationship with My Father

My father and I never really had a close relationship. I can remember times as a child when he would pick me up and take me horseback riding. I can also remember times when he was supposed to pick me up and I sat waiting looking out of the window all day but he never showed. He always told me that my mother was the reason he did not show up and I believed him; that caused me to resent my mother because I thought she was keeping me from my father. I later discovered that my mother was not keeping me from him, there were other reasons he did not show.

There was a brief time when I was in the sixth grade that I lived with my father for six months. During those six months there were good times and bad times; just like any household, but at the end of those six months; my time with him ended. After those six months ended, I did not see my father or hear from him much.

My Hope Deflated

June 26, 1994, the night I was shot, my father did show up at the hospital to see me. After that night I did not see him again until February 14, 1995, when I was placed in the hospital in Selma, Alabama waiting to be transferred to a nursing home. I was in the hospital in Selma for 30 days and my father visited me every day. Those 30 days were the most my father and I had ever communicated and the closest we had ever been to one another. Seeing him walk through that door every day was the highlight of my day; it brought me joy and gave me hope. I was sure my father was going to take me home with him and care for me, but he did not.

On March 15, 1995, the last day I was there, my father stood up, looked me in my eyes and said, "Son, no matter how much you love something or someone there comes a time when you have to let go" and he turned around and walked out of the room. He never came to see me again after that day.

When my father walked out of that room it was as if someone stuck a needle inside of a balloon; I was deflated of all hope. At that moment, a deep hatred entered my heart for my father. I remember thinking that I hated him and would never forgive him for what he had done.

On March 15, 1995, I was transferred to a nursing home in Tuskegee, Alabama, where I stayed for two years and then to another nursing home in Montgomery, Alabama where I stayed for 3 months and 5 days. I had not seen or heard from my father during that time and, honestly, the thoughts of him were not as strong anymore. Then one day the strangest thing happened; I was sitting in the back of the nursing home in Montgomery when the husband of one of the nurses started talking with me. I told him I was from Marion, and he said, "I know a guy from Marion and his name is Lorenzo also; he drives big trucks." I replied, "That's my father." He said, "I see your father three or four days a week down the road from here. Does he know you're here?" I replied, "He knows I am in a nursing home but I don't know if he knows I am in this specific one." He said, "I am certain I will see your father tomorrow and I am going to tell him you're here."

A few days later, the man came back. He said, "I saw your father and told him you were here. He said he was coming to see you; did he come?" I replied, "No, he did not." He never did come to see me and all of the hatred, anger and bitterness I had toward my father resurfaced again.

The Moment I Forgave My Father

On Fathers' Day of 2004, the Lord moved my heart with compassion for my father. I had not seen or heard from him since March 15, 1995. The last words I remember him saying were, "Son no matter how much you love something or someone, there comes a time when you have to let go." The last time I saw him, he was walking out of my hospital room while I laid flat on my back in a hospital bed. Nine years of no communication then the Lord moved my heart with compassion to call him.

I knew he stayed in Fort Wayne, Indiana so I got online and found three people with his name in Fort Wayne. On the second call his wife answered; she instantly knew who I was.

She gave my father the phone, he answered and said, "Hey son what made you call?" I replied and said, "Happy Father's Day" I went on to say, "I know we have not had a good relationship but I would like to put that behind us and see if we can have a father–son relationship; would you like that?" He replied and said, "Yes, I would."

For months, we talked three or four times a week, and he even made a couple of trips to Birmingham to see me; it was great! After he saw the progress I had made in life, he began to ask me for money; I then realized his motives were wrong so the relationship did not last.

In January of 2008, my father died. I am so glad he did not die before I forgave him. Now I can live in peace without any regrets. If you are at odds with a parent, forgive them. It does not matter what they said or did, or how much anger, bitterness and resentment you have toward them, forgive them even if you cannot have a relationship with them. When you forgive, you can live in peace without any regrets.

A THOUGHT TO TAKE

It is wrong to withhold forgiveness because you feel that someone doesn't deserve it. Forgiveness does not need to be earned before it can be given.

Chapter 5

Forgiving My Family and Friends

....

Colossians 3:13

Bearing with one another, and forgiving one another, if anyone has a complaint against another; even as Christ forgave you, so you also must do.

Don't live your life with anger and hate in your heart. You'll only be hurting yourself more than the people you hate. – Unknown

I cannot say that we have ever had a very close-knit family but I never imagined I would experience a crisis of such magnitude and my family and friends would not be there for support. Regardless of whether your family is close or not, some things are expected. A person expects their family and friends to be there for them during a crisis.

In the beginning of my paralysis various family members and friends visited me regularly in the hospital. The visits were short-lived and then no one came to visit. When I was released to come home from the hospital in November of 1994 no one was home; someone had to go find my mother to let her know that I was home. The house had no heat, running water or working appliances. None of my family members or friends made an offer for me to come to their homes where there was heat, running water and working appliances, neither did they offer to get the heat or water turned on; no one cared.

As I explained earlier, my thirteen-year-old brother, Alonzo, was my primary care provider. My mother was on drugs and alcohol; my father was not there and none of my other family members or friends cared enough to even come by to help. I hated them for not being there; I hated them for not caring.

I was Crushed

The mother of my first-born children and I were young when we met. She was 12 and I was 13, we were two young kids with a lot going on in our lives. Her father died when she was younger; my father and I had no relationship and we both had unstable homes. I guess we found meaning in one another. At the time of my paralysis she was 16 and I was 17 and we had two-month-old twin daughters. That was a very complicated set of circumstances for two teenagers. Two months after I was injured, one of our twin daughters died; that complicated life even more.

The first five months of my paralysis, she was there. She was at the hospital as often as she could be, and when I came home, she was there helping as much as she could. One afternoon she told me that she was going to her mother's house and would be back the next day to see me. When the next day came, she did not come back; she never came back again; I was crushed.

I sent message after message asking if she would come to see me but she would not. Several times I had someone transfer me from my wheelchair into their car and take me to her house. I would sit outside of her house for hours begging her to please come out to see me but she would not. During one of my greatest times of need in my life, she abandoned me just like everyone else and I hated her for it.

Where Was Everyone When I Needed Them

I was in two different nursing homes for 2 years 3 months and 5 days, and the entire time I was there, I never received a visit from a family member or loved one; I was totally abandoned. I initiated phone calls to my family regularly. The only way I could call was collect. I will never forget the day, when I made a collect call to my family and found out that collect calls had been blocked. It was devastating to find that the only way of communicating with my family had been cut off.

I felt completely thrown away the day I found out those collect calls were blocked. I was in a nursing home in Tuskegee, Alabama hundreds of miles from anyone I knew, surrounded by unfamiliar people and unfamiliar things; paralyzed from my chest down to my feet. All I kept thinking was, "Why won't they visit me? Why won't anyone call? Why would they block my calls?" Every thought infuriated me more and more. The hatred for my family and friends was deeply rooted inside of me.

They Called Me in Their Time of Need

As I shared in Chapter Two, the Lord miraculously moved in my life, delivered me out of the nursing home, and captured my heart. After getting out of the nursing home, I went to a Transitional Living Unit in Birmingham, Alabama where I was trained to independently live on my own.

On May 3, 1999, my brother, Alonzo and I moved into a house together. Alonzo is the same brother who primarily cared for me when he was 13-years-old. At 18, he became my primary care giver again. He cared for me night and day for eight years; no outside agencies ever came in. Alonzo was the only family member that was there in my time of need. I do not know where my life would be today if it were not for Alonzo.

Life significantly improved; and when it did, those same family members and friends who were not there for me in my time of need began calling me to help them with their problems. It is amazing how the Lord can turn things around.

Instead of Hurting, I Helped

There I was, being called on for help by the exact people who completely abandoned me. It would have been the perfect opportunity to hurt them just as badly as they had hurt me. I could have had my revenge, but instead of hurting them; I helped them. All of the hatred that was deep rooted inside of me for them was no longer in my heart. It was no longer there because of the love Christ had shown me.

Being abandoned by those you love and who are supposed to love you, brings a pain that is difficult to fathom. Abandonment will create a deep root of hatred inside your heart. Thoughts of hurting them; making them feel the pain they made you feel will consume you. When the opportunity arises to hurt them just as bad as they hurt you, do not take it. Instead, use that opportunity to forgive them.

A THOUGHT TO TAKE

When you're given the opportunity to hurt someone that has hurt you; don't take it. Forgiveness is more liberating than revenge.

Chapter 6

Forgiving God

....

Daniel 9:9

To the Lord our God belong mercy and forgiveness, though
we have rebelled against Him.

God has forgiven me and has enabled me to forgive others. How can I not love a God who loves me in this way? – Lorenzo T. Brown

If you have ever been touched by tragedy, then chances are you have felt hurt or been disappointed by God. Some of the questions you have probably asked are, "God why didn't you intervene? Why didn't you stop it? Why didn't you help? How could you let them die? How could you let them leave? How could you let this happen? God why?"

Because of our faith in God, we expect Him to show up during a time of tragedy. When it appears that He will not we can feel abandoned by God. "God, you said you would never leave me or forsake me" (Deut. 31:6), but when I needed you, you were not there. Feeling abandoned by God can cause us to become offended with God.

When we are offended with God, it damages our relationship with Him. The offense causes us to walk away from God. We abandon our faith in Him because we feel He has abandoned us; we refuse to attend church, read His word, pray or continue to acknowledge His existence.

"Our thoughts are not His thoughts; our ways are not His ways" (Isaiah 55:8-9). Our human minds will never understand why God allows certain things to occur in this life that causes us pain. I was offended with God because I could not understand why a loving God would let me experience so much pain and the offense damaged my relationship with God.

It took some time, but God found His way back into my heart. My heart is now 100% free of any offense toward God; I have forgiven God. I now see that despite the pain that I went through, God never left me. He was there the entire time; He did not abandon me.

If you are in a place of pain in your life and you feel that God has abandoned you, I empathize with you. But, I want you to know that God will never leave you or forsake you. You may not feel His presence because of the pain, but He is with you. God has not abandoned you.

I Was So Angry With God

I was so angry with God! I felt that my life had been very difficult and unfair. My mother was a drug addict and an alcoholic, my father did not care about me, my family and friends did not care, my daughter died, the men who shot me were free, and I was left paralyzed from my chest down to my feet laying in a nursing home at the age of eighteen.

I had been completely abandoned by everyone that I loved and I felt as if God had abandoned me too. I opened my mouth and I screamed as loud as I could, "God, I hate you!

What kind of loving God could let me live like this? Why don't you just let me die?"

I Asked God to Heal Me

I prayed many times and asked God to heal me. I asked Him to restore my feeling and movement; to reverse the effects of my paralysis. I believed in my heart that God could do anything and when He did not heal me, I was extremely angry with Him.

I watched others who were paralyzed walk again, God had healed them; why was He not healing me? I do not know the answer to why God chose not to physically heal me. To be honest with you, having the answer to that question is no longer important to me. Here is what I do know. "There is nothing impossible with God" (Luke 1:37). I still believe He can do anything. If God chooses not to physically heal, it is not because He cannot; it is because He has a greater purpose for you. Yes, a purpose greater than physical healing!

It is because of my paralysis that I have been used by Christ to touch the lives of others in ways that I never would have if I were not paralyzed. Yes, walking again would be a miracle, but living a life free of hatred, anger, bitterness and resentment; with a heart filled with love, joy and forgiveness is also a miracle!

God healed my heart, He enabled me to forgive people that I thought I could never forgive and to forgive them for things that I thought were unforgivable. Healing occurs in different ways. A person with an unhealed heart lives in greater bondage than a person with an unhealed body.

I do not have to be healed physically to love God and you do not either. God does not love you any less than the person who He physically healed. More important than physical healing is our relationship with Him; do not let anything stand in the way of that.

Why my Mother? – Why my Father? – Why my Family?

"Why did my mother have to be a drug addict and alcoholic? Why wasn't my dad in my life? Why was my family so unstable?" I asked God these questions over and over again. How could God love me when He gave me parents and a family like that?

I hated God because my mother was a drug addict and an alcoholic, because my dad was not in my life and because my family was unstable. I could not understand why He was not answering my prayers and delivering my mother from her addiction. Why was He not making my father love me? Why was He not bringing my family together? Surely, God knows that my life would be better if I had better parents and a better family.

Unfortunately, many people have unfit parents and unstable families. We cannot control the decisions our parents and families make; we can only control our decisions. Whatever is going on in our parents and families lives is a decision they chose; it is not God's fault.

I came to learn that I could not make a decision to hate God because of the parents and family I had and you cannot either. Even if our parents are unfit and our families are unstable, God still loves us. *"When my father and my mother forsake me, then the Lord will take care of me" (Psalm 27:10).*

God Was Working the Entire Time

I had it hard all of my life and at the age of 17, I was paralyzed from my chest down, living in a nursing home. My family abandoned me, one of my daughters died, and the men who shot me were free. "God where were you? Why did this happen to me? This isn't fair!!!"

It seemed like God was on everyone's side except mine. I just could not see the hand of God in all of it. I hated God for what He allowed to happen in my life. If He was such a loving and powerful God, then where was He? "Why didn't He help me?"

What I did not know was that when I was going through all of the pain and suffering in my life, God was at work in my life the entire time. Everything I went through as a child because of my mother's addiction, God was at work in my life. Everything I went through because my father was not there, God was at work in my life. Everything I went through because my family and friends had abandoned me, God was at work in my life. Everything I went through because of my paralysis, God was at work in my life. Nothing about pain is pleasant and we will never understand why God permits it. But, God is not absent from any part of our lives that involves pain and suffering; He is right there; working in it.

My pain has now become my platform. Everything that I went through is now the very thing that God works through in my life and ministry. None of it was in vain! No, life was not fair but I would not change one thing if it would prevent me from knowing the love of God the way that I now know it.

The day will come when the very thing that brings you the greatest pain will be the very thing that God uses in the greatest way in your life. Nothing you are currently experiencing is in vain; God is working in it!

To Those Who Love Him

After I forgave God and turned my heart back toward Him my life changed. All of the heartache and pain I experienced came together for good in my life. Turn your heart back toward God; He can cause all of your heartache and pain to come together for good in your life.

"And we know that all things work together for good to those who love God, to those who are the called according to His purpose" (Romans 8:28). There is a key portion of this scripture that I would like you to focus on *"to those who love God."* Do you love God? Or is there hatred, anger, bitterness and resentment in your heart that is preventing you from loving Him? Unforgiveness toward God can prevent all things from working together for good in your life. Forgiveness causes it all to work together for good.

Have You Forgiven God

The fact that you even feel hurt by God is truth that you love Him, because you cannot feel hurt by someone that you do not love. I know it is difficult to turn your heart back toward God after feeling that He has abandoned you. But God is the only one who can mend your heart and take away the pain.

God knows the thoughts and plans that He has for your life (Jeremiah 29:11). Those thoughts and plans do not change or end because you are experiencing some unwanted pain. He does not remove Himself from you when you are hurting; He draws closer to you.

Because of the pain you are feeling, you pushed Him away and turned your back on Him. He never pushed you away or turned His back on you. He is still in the same place you left Him waiting with open arms for you to return to Him. It is time for you to let go of the unforgiveness you have in your heart toward God and forgive Him.

Check your heart; cleanse it of any hatred, anger, bitterness, and resentment that you have toward God. God loves you! He gave His only begotten Son so that you would not perish. *(John 3:16) For God so loved the world that He gave His only begotten Son, that whoever believes in Him should not perish but have everlasting life.* Do not let unforgiveness prevent you from experiencing this love.

A THOUGHT TO TAKE

Unforgiveness holds us in bondage! Don't let unforgiveness prevent you from experiencing the joy of living without animosity.

Closing Words

....

During the writing of this book, the Lord tested my heart. My wife and I loaned a family member who was financially struggling, a large sum of money. We all agreed that they would pay us back $200 a month. Month after month, there was an excuse as to why they were unable to give us anything. By the end of six months, we had only received a total of $55.

Whenever we would ask for our money, they would say rude things to us and make us appear to be bad people for asking. It got to the point that whenever I would see the person, I would feel animosity in my heart for them. One day, my wife and I were out for a drive and I shared with her what I was feeling in my heart. My wife said that she was feeling the same way in her heart.

That day, we decided that we would rather forgive the debt than to live with animosity in our hearts. Our family was not in a financial situation where we were able to forgive a debt that large, but a greater debt was at stake for us; the debt of unforgiveness. Unforgiveness could possibly be the one thing that holds more people in bondage than anything else.

On New Year's Eve, 2014, I texted the family member and told them that we forgave the debt and they no longer needed to pay us back. After sending that text, a burden was lifted; suddenly I felt free. Animosity is a heavy thing to live with.

I was driving around town the same day I sent the text when I heard the Lord say to me, "Why waste your time hating someone, when you can invest your time loving them? Hate will not reward you in anyway, but love will reward you in every way!"

ACKNOWLEDGEMENTS

....

I want to give a special thanks to my wife, April. Words cannot express how grateful I am for the sacrifices that you make on a daily basis for our children and myself. I thank God for blessing me with you. You are the greatest wife that a man could ever ask for.

Secondly, my three beautiful children; Marilyn, Isaac and Isaiah. You guys fill my days with laughter and my heart with joy. You are my motivation!

Your love and support means everything to me.

Questions and Topics for Discussion

. . . .

I had an opportunity to get revenge, but I chose not to take it. If you had an opportunity to get revenge on someone who hurt you, would you take it?

Is revenge ever justified?

My niece was murdered and we forgave the people who murdered her. I forgave the men involved with the shooting that left me paralyzed and, I forgave my family and friends for not being there. Would you forgive acts like these?

Can anything or anyone be forgiven?

Should forgiveness be withheld in certain situations?

I never received an apology from those who hurt me but I still extended forgiveness to them. Should a person apologize before they are forgiven?

Is an apology necessary in order to forgive?

I have forgiven everyone who has caused me pain but I still can remember everything that happened. Does forgiveness mean you are going to forget?

Have you truly forgiven if you have not forgotten what happened?

Even though I forgave my father, we still were not able to reconcile our relationship. Is reconciliation required in order to forgive?

Does forgiveness benefit you or the other person more?

Are you choosing not to forgive because you feel that if you forgive you are doing the other person a favor or letting them off the hook?

Matthew 6:9-15

In this manner, therefore, pray: Our Father in heaven, Hallowed be Your name. Your kingdom come. Your will be done on earth as it is in heaven. Give us this day our daily bread. And forgive us our debts, as we forgive our debtors. And do not lead us into temptation, but deliver us from the evil one. For Yours is the kingdom and the power and the glory forever. Amen.

"For if you forgive men their trespasses, your Heavenly Father will also forgive you. But if you do not forgive men their trespasses, neither will your Father forgive your trespasses."

MOVING BEYOND THE OFFENSE

MOVING BEYOND THE OFFENSE

_____

_____

_____

_____

_____

_____

_____

_____

_____

_____

_____

_____

_____

_____

_____

_____

_____

_____

MOVING BEYOND THE OFFENSE

MOVING BEYOND THE OFFENSE

MOVING BEYOND THE OFFENSE

_____

_____

_____

_____

_____

_____

_____

_____

_____

_____

_____

_____

_____

_____

_____

_____

_____

_____

MOVING BEYOND THE OFFENSE

_____

_____

_____

_____

_____

_____

_____

_____

_____

_____

_____

_____

_____

_____

_____

_____

_____

_____

_____

_____

MOVING BEYOND THE OFFENSE

MOVING BEYOND THE OFFENSE

_____

_____

_____

_____

_____

_____

_____

_____

_____

_____

_____

_____

_____

_____

_____

_____

_____

_____

MOVING BEYOND THE OFFENSE

_____

_____

_____

_____

_____

_____

_____

_____

_____

_____

_____

_____

_____

_____

_____

_____

_____

_____

_____

MOVING BEYOND THE OFFENSE

_____

_____

_____

_____

_____

_____

_____

_____

_____

_____

_____

_____

_____

_____

_____

_____

_____

_____

_____

_____

MOVING BEYOND THE OFFENSE

MOVING BEYOND THE OFFENSE

_____

_____

_____

_____

_____

_____

_____

_____

_____

_____

_____

_____

_____

_____

_____

_____

_____

_____

_____

_____

_____

_____

_____

_____

_____

_____

_____

_____

_____

_____

_____

_____

_____

_____

_____

_____

_____